Presented to:

Becky

With love from:

Alissa + Chris Moss

Date

9/13/14

This book was given to us at a time when we need some encouragement. You have been through a lot lately. I hope this book brings you much well. God loves you so much & he wants you well.

Love you,
Alissa
Chris Moss

Love,
Sheri
Austin

GOD'S CAR WASH

Faith, Hope and Buckets of Soap

By Sheri Austin

DEDICATION

My Parents
Lee and Elfie Jacobs

Thank you for your love, support and adopting me! God has been blessing me since the day you brought me home from the hospital. Your marriage has been a source of inspiration to me. I'm forever grateful for the amazing life you both have given me. Dad, thank you for rolling all those quarters from the car wash, you made my life so much better. I appreciate how you always said "can't doesn't live here" - your constant encouragement gave me the confidence to follow my dreams. You are such a dedicated godly man, husband and father. Mom, you are one heck of a bodyguard and my best friend. God demonstrated his love for me through your love every day. Thank you for the godly home, heritage and for always supporting and believing in me.

Jeff and Steven

You guys have brought so much joy to my life. Even though we've been through some very tough times you both have stayed strong and inspired those around you by your faith in God. I'm excited to watch the plans of the Lord unfold in your lives. My greatest gift in life is being your Mom.

Sarah

Love brought us together as a family and sadly death has tried to keep us apart. I am proud of your accomplishments and your love for teaching others. I pray that you know you are loved. The world tells us that time heals all wounds. The truth is only Jesus can heal our wounds and our broken heart.

In memory of James Austin

Thank you for your love and dedication to our family. You worked so hard for so many years. I have always said "you crammed one hundred years into forty nine years." You were taken from us way too soon. I'm so glad you met Jesus through our journey together. I am a better woman for knowing and loving you.

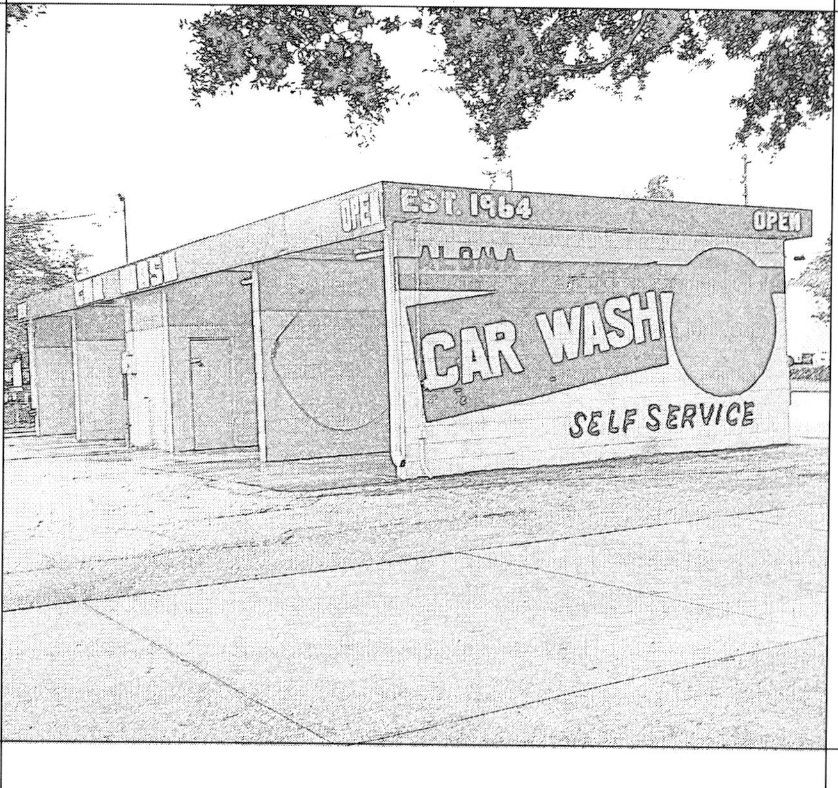
OPEN
EST. 1964
OPEN
CAR WASH
SELF SERVICE

PROLOGUE

In 1998, my husband, Jim and I became the proud business owners of a self-service car wash in Winter Park, Florida. We both worked for the local phone company for over 15 years when we decided that it would be a good time to purchase the car wash and add one more thing to our over scheduled lives in suburbia.

Nine years after the purchase of our business, I found myself alone to raise my kids and run the car wash after Jim lost his battle to cancer. I have had some incredible encounters with God and some supernatural experiences at my little car wash. One Christmas morning, I was sharing a story with my boys how God had blessed me with the gifts from the car wash that I was about to give my son Jeff, when my youngest son Steven said "That car wash is like a portal from heaven!" He's absolutely right; the car wash is like a portal from heaven.

The good news is that you don't have to be at my car wash to experience the love of God or a portal from heaven. God has already expressed his love to us through the gift of his son, Jesus. We already have everything we need for this life through our relationship with Jesus. It sounds like a lofty and spiritual statement but it's the truth. The problem is that we have so many distractions in this world. Strife at home, neck-breaking after school schedules and conflict rob us of the peace and joy God wants us to experience. We are unconsciously choosing death over life by the words we speak, the things we participate in and just being way too busy.

God wants to express his love for you in countless ways. I hope that this little book of signs, wonders and the valuable life lessons from my personal life and crazy car wash stories will increase your faith and your hope in Jesus. Life brings much heartbreak and challenges because we live in a fallen world. God is a good God. Jesus wants to equip us to overcome the trials that we face from our adversary and experience his kingdom on earth as it is in heaven. If your life is messy and dirty you have picked up the right book for faith and hope. Your life, like your car can never get too dirty, broken down or messy for God. God is in the restoration business. He makes all things new again. No matter what you are facing in life - I pray that your heart will be open to the truth and promises of God's word. We serve a loving God who is very mindful of all the things that concern you. Faith and hope will increase when you put your trust in him alone. Nothing in this world satisfies like Jesus and no one will ever love you more than he does.

FORWARD

By Cristy Pennell

Can messages from God be found at a car wash? You know signs of his presence? An "atta boy", a wink, a nod, an "I got this for you" an "I'm rooting for you?" You bet!

In the seemingly mundane, wet, messy, lint-filled depths of a do-it-yourself car wash in Winter Park, Florida, God prevails. No, you're not going to see visions, or pilgrims looking for heavenly signs from above. You won't hear herald angel trumpets or see Jesus' face etched on your windshield. You'll find God in vacuum hoses, trash cans, curbs and folks looking to get bird poop off their vehicles. And, boy does God delight in showing up in all kinds of funny situations.

God's Car Wash – Faith, Hope and Buckets of Soap takes us on author Sheri Austin's many escapades in running this business, from the time she took it over with her late husband, Jim, to the business' eventual sale. It's been such an interesting vehicle (pun intended) that can be seen as a direct dialogue between Sheri and God as her personal relationship with Jesus really began to help Sheri hear, feel and see God's goodness.

This charming little book is full of uplifting stories of validation, triumph and small but significant signs that God leaves for us to show us he's with us and wants to give us the desires of our hearts. From the perfect size and color sweatshirt, to the luxury items God gave Sheri to give to her son one Christmas … you just have to read these anecdotes to know that we have a God of purpose, not coincidence. He is so eager to meet us wherever we are. He'll even hang out with us at a car wash!

Just invite him in and see for yourself how God works in your life when you're open to receiving his messages of hope and encouragement and his gifts of friendship and love. God is everywhere! God's Car Wash – Faith, Hope and Buckets of Soap is a great example of God's goodness and love.

TABLE OF CONTENTS

God Knows Your Desires .... Page 17

Silver Cross .... Page 19

Be Bold .... Page 23

Parenting With A Purpose .... Page 27

A Matter of Faith .... Page 31

Do Not Be Afraid .... Page 35

Angels Among Us .... Page 39

Ask and Receive .... Page 43

Fire! .... Page 47

Wisdom .... Page 51

Tithe to Ties .... Page 55

Are You Who You Want To Be? .... Page 59

You Are Loved .... Page 63

Blessed .... Page 67

3:16 .... Page 71

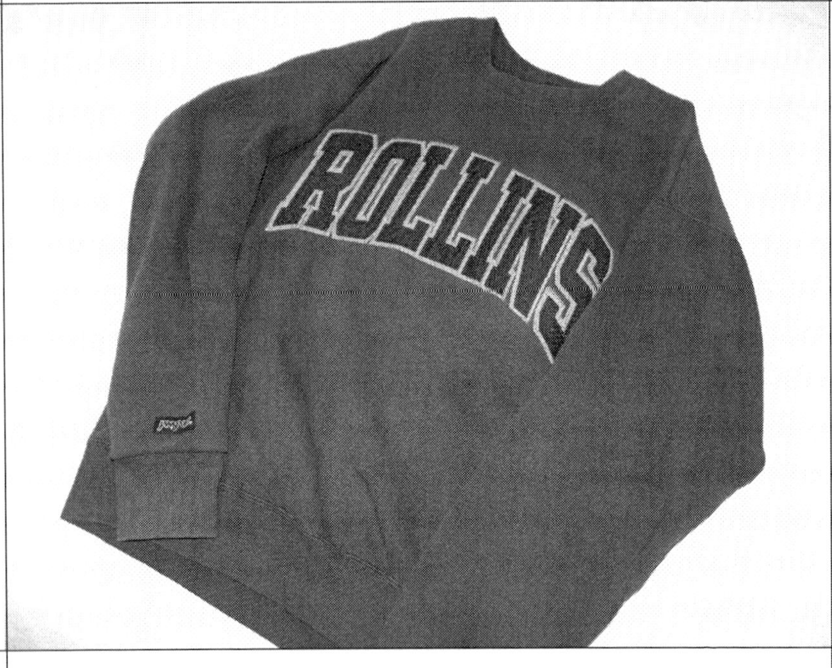
ROLLINS

GOD KNOWS YOUR DESIRES

Delight yourself in the Lord and He will give you the desires of your heart.
– Psalm 37:4

It's easy to get so caught up in all the things that we have to do each day, that we can quickly forget that God sees us and our struggles. God knows our heart and desires. There was a time in my life when I was busy taking care of three children, my husband, working full time by day and by night my husband and I would take care of our self-service car wash. I was a worn out and weary woman.

Do you ever wonder if God sees you or if he really cares? Is the Creator of the Universe really mindful of me? Psalm 139:1-4 states "O Lord, you have searched me and you know me. You know when I sit and when I rise; you perceive my thoughts from afar. You discern my going out and my lying down; you are familiar with all my ways. Before a word is on my tongue you know it completely, O Lord." God does see you; he knows your heart and desires. He cares for you and loves you with an everlasting love.

I was fortunate to attend and graduate from Rollins College, located just a couple miles from my little car wash. I owned one sweatshirt from my college days. We really don't have that many weeks of cold weather to contend with in the Sunshine State, our winter clothes will go out of style long before they will wear out. My Rollins sweatshirt looked a little frayed and I really wanted a new college sweatshirt for Christmas. When I told my husband about my Christmas wish for a new sweatshirt, he chuckled and said "That's it? Is that all you want?" "Yep, that's all I want". Then I forgot about it. Honestly, I didn't think my husband would buy me one. Jim always bought big ticket items for the kids and me at Christmas. The odds were not in my favor for getting a new Rollins sweatshirt for Christmas.

One brisk Saturday morning, we were doing our normal routine at the car wash, by collecting money, cleaning out the bays and dumping the trash. Jim and I would divide the business in half he would take the right side of the business and I would work the left side. As I was approaching the next garbage can to dump, (the heavens opened, angels sang, harps played, and bells chimed-well maybe in heaven) on the curb was a beautiful forest green Rollins College sweatshirt with big navy letters in mint condition. God even knows my color palate! God loves me so much! A grey sweatshirt would be okay, but a forest green color is perfect. God is perfect.

Friend, God is in the details of every aspect of our life if we invite him. I truly believe he knew that my husband was not going to get me the desires of my heart even if it was a simple sweatshirt for Christmas. God loves us so much and he wants to give his children good gifts. It wasn't until several years later that I would realize how much God loves me and wants to have a relationship with me.

David wrote in Psalm 20:4 "May he give you the desires of your heart and make all your plans succeed." Our heavenly Father wants to give his children the desires of their heart and he also wants all our plans to succeed. I love that word "all." God doesn't just want some of our plans to prosper but all of our plans prosper. I've learned that when we truly delight in Jesus, follow the Holy Spirit and his commands, God not only will give us the desires of our hearts he will lovingly guide us to fulfill the plans that he has for us when we trust and follow him. Your Abba Father loves you so much. God wants to shower you with some unexpected gifts along the way too.

SILVER CROSS

This is how we know what love is: Jesus Christ laid down his life for us.
– 1 John 3:16a

On that beautiful cross Jesus poured out his love to the world by paying our debt for all our sins. Past, present and future sins are forgiven. That's an amazing gift and great news! Jesus has defeated the enemy and he bought and paid for our healing, prosperity and salvation on the cross. 1 Peter 2:24 tells us that "He himself bore our sins in his body on the cross, so that we might die to sins and live for righteousness; by his wounds you have been healed." The cross symbolizes what Jesus did for you and me.

Over the years while working at the car wash we've found missing family heirlooms, sunglasses, toys and lots of change. You'd be surprised at how much money and Cheerios gets sucked into vacuums, not to mention all the pennies that just get tossed on the ground. One day at the car wash, my husband found a beautiful silver cross in one of the vacuums. Jim believed in God, but wasn't convinced that Jesus was who he claimed to be.

When Jim found the cross, he eagerly brought it to me like a little boy who had just found a buried treasure. He excitedly, said, "Look what I found for you!" I thought to myself, found for me? You found it; God intended for you to find it. I kept my superior spiritual thoughts to myself. (PS Pride is so very ugly) and said "Wow that is great." I didn't have pockets so I tucked the cross into my bra, not the safest place, but that was my only option at the time.

By the time we got home, I discovered that I had lost the cross. Up to this point in my life, God for over ten years had been reaching my heart with various signs and God winks. I know that God has been with me from day one. When I was a young Mom at a very low point in my life, I was struggling in my previous marriage and had been seeking the Lord and praying for a sign as to what to do in my marriage. Life didn't appear to be improving at all even after several months of praying and attending a codependency support group at Northland Church. I was growing very impatient, weary and frustrated.

One morning as I was driving to my Grandmother's house I cried out to the Lord, "Please Lord, give me a sign." My life was in a horrible pit. I was facing divorce and being a single parent. My sweet little son Jeffrey was a toddler and he was losing his Daddy. Alcoholism was spinning our life out of control. Later that morning at my Grandmother's house, I was helping Jeffrey toddle up her front walkway when I found a shiny sticker with praying hands in her front yard. Honestly, at that time in my life, my attitude matched my maturity level with the Lord. Not only was I disappointed but I wanted a solution to my problems from God right then. God on the other hand wanted me to keep praying and to trust him.

The scriptures tell us to pray without ceasing. I know that truth now, but I didn't know that truth twenty years ago. Keep praying friend because if it's not good, it's not over. God will work it out for our good. Losing the cross that Jim had found was pretty disappointing. The very next day after I lost the cross, I found it, shining brightly in the parking lot of the car wash. Finding that cross was a sweet little gift and reminder from God. Jesus loves me and he loves you. He promises to never leave or forsake us. The cross represents God's unfailing love for the world. God gave his son Jesus to save us from our sin, give us eternal life, to heal our bodies, renew our minds and to have an abundant life on earth.

Sometimes we get off track; we fail, walk away from the Lord or lose our way. We all face tough times in life. Once you call on the Lord for his help, he will be your ever present helper. Remember, that you may be the only one who is seeking the Lord for help or guidance for the challenge that you are facing. It will take time for the hearts and minds of others to be changed. Be patient. Trust in the Lord, especially in his timing and in the power of prayer.

I've learned that no matter what life brings, if you are broken hearted, facing many troubles or you have strayed from God, his love for us never fails. His love for us is unconditional. David wrote in Psalm 34:17 "The righteous cry out, and the Lord hears them. He delivers them from all their troubles. The Lord is close to the broken hearted and saves those who are crushed in spirit. A righteous man may have many troubles, but the Lord delivers him from them all…" You can't earn his love, it's a free gift. Receive the amazing love God has for you! Jesus has paid for your salvation, health, prosperity, peace and sins on that wonderful cross. Jesus is waiting with arms wide open for you to come to him and trust him with your whole heart. I encourage you to run into his loving arms.

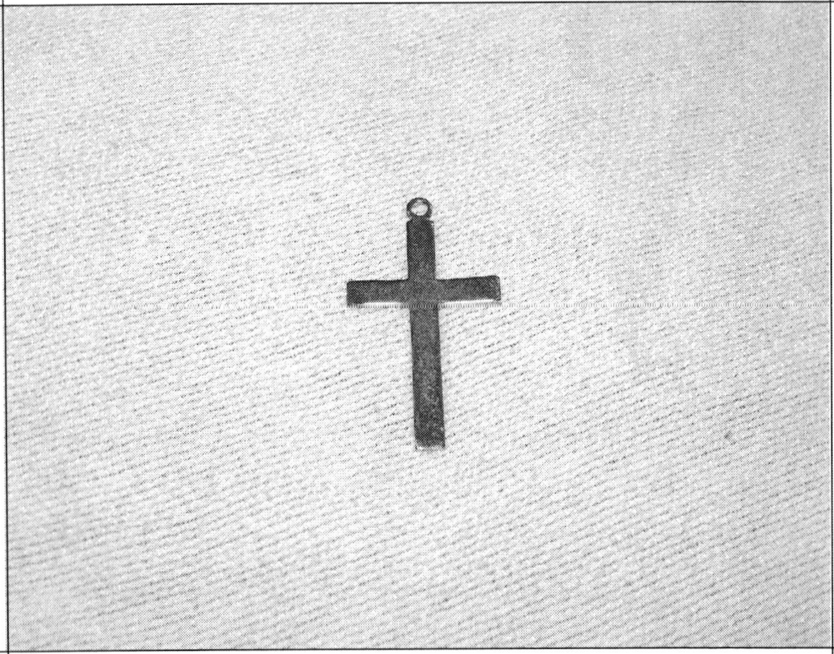

BE BOLD

Now, Lord, consider their threats and enable your servants to speak your word with great boldness. – Acts 4:29

I think I've become bolder with age, but to be perfectly honest I was such a cry baby when I was younger. My Dad would just have to give me "the look" and the water works would start. I have matured with the help of the Holy Spirit. I don't get upset so easily or offended over the slightest thing like I use to. One of the amazing things that happen when you become born again, the Holy Spirit starts the renovation process in our lives.

You don't have to get it all together to come to Jesus. Heck, I still don't have it all together, but I sure do like what he's done in my life so far and he's not done with me yet. The restoration and renovation process can be slow and exhausting on our own. As I studied the scriptures and sought Jesus daily, I discovered the renovation process can actually be less complicated when we are led by the Spirit.

The Holy Spirit can restore our broken or anxious heart and he can renovate us into more than we ever dreamed possible. When I look back at my life, I was actually quite shy in my youth. As time marched on, God moved me into various roles of leadership which has prepared me for the path he has me on now. God will do the same with you. He wants to mold us to be bold, live in the authority and power Jesus died for us to have. The great news is that as you renew your mind with the truth of God's word, your spirit, soul and body will grow stronger.

The scriptures are so powerful. They are sharper than a double-edged sword. The Word of God when applied will cut through any situation and give you the wisdom you need. Hebrews 4:12 tells us that "For the Word of God is alive and active. Sharper than any double-edged sword, it penetrates even to dividing soul and spirit, joints and marrow; it judges the thoughts and attitudes of the heart." The Word of God will go right to your heart and your spirit. It will also bring healing to your bones. Acts 4:29 is one of my favorite scriptures "Now, Lord, consider their threats and enable your servants to speak your word with great boldness." Have you ever been threatened? I have. It's amazing when you are filled with the power of the Holy Spirit and you know the Word of God, you're equipped to stand firm and speak with great boldness. I have always been non-confrontational; truth be known I've been a "people pleaser" for many years, to a fault. Life has dished out several occasions where thankfully God put boldness and even a holy fighter in me to stand for the truth found in the Bible.

I stood firm and boldly confronted the woman who was having an affair with my husband. I was a wreck with him and so hurt, but I was not about to stand by and watch a stranger come in and destroy us. Even though my flesh wanted to pound on her; I told her that I would be fighting for my marriage and would not be leaving my husband. Keeping my family together for my children gave me my strength and resolve to fight for my marriage. Nehemiah 4:14 was the double-edged sword I needed for the fight of my life. "Don't be afraid of them. Remember the Lord, who is great and awesome, and fight for your families, your sons and your daughters, your wives and your homes." I had God on my side! God is great and awesome and I had to trust him every second of those heart breaking eleven months.

I had several face to face encounters with the "other woman", God put a holy fight in my spirit and God's girl won that tough battle. It wasn't easy. Jesus said we would have trouble in this world. He tells us to not let our hearts be troubled because he has overcome the world. We can overcome too. Acts 4:30 tells us to take action and "Stretch out your hand to heal and perform signs and wonders through the name of your holy servant Jesus." We not only need to speak the name of Jesus, but let's start expecting signs and wonders in his mighty name. Let's speak the Word of God with great boldness, with stretched out hands in faith to touch those who need healing through the power of Jesus that is working in us.

I've learned that when we know in our hearts that God goes before us, he is with us and will be our rear guard, there is nothing to fear. Let's start being bolder and speak the Word of God in love to those who need to hear the good news of the gospel. Let's be brave and believe that God heals through the mighty name of Jesus when we boldly proclaim that by his stripes we are healed and that he sent forth his word and healed their bodies. He can heal our relationships too. We truly have all we need in Christ Jesus. Let's be bold and start sharing the good news of Jesus Christ.

PARENTING WITH A PURPOSE

> *This day I call the heavens and the earth as witnesses against you that I have set before you life and death, blessings and curses. Now choose life, so that you and your children may live. – Deuteronomy 30:19*

God tells us that he has set before us, life or death, blessings and curses. Are you choosing life for you and your family or are your choices and lifestyle bringing death to your life and loved ones? Back in 2004, our church was just starting home groups to meet and participate in the Purpose Driven Life movement. At the onset of this exciting time in our church, I received an anonymous letter in the mail that suggested my husband was involved with a woman where we both worked. The claim of his infidelity was backed up with proof from cell phone records. Behind my happy mask, my world was crumbling right in front of this home group that had only been meeting for a few weeks. Our diverse home group comprised of some of my co-workers and their spouses as well as some older church couples.

Every week I showed up alone because home groups were not for Jim. I participated in the group but was suffering silently because I didn't want anyone to know what was going on in my marriage. The cloak of shame was so heavy and suffocating. Over that six week period of our home group meetings, I was bombarded almost daily at work with tormenting messages on post-it notes that were left on my desk. Letters spelling my husband's infidelity were sent to me in the inter-company mail from a bystander that was watching my husband's every move. The work place harassment was brutal.

I continued to participate in the Purpose Driven Life home group but I was dying inside. I tried to keep it all together emotionally and professionally. Hiding my feelings from my home group was relatively easy but trying to hide my pain from my children and my parents was extremely difficult and exhausting. The morning of our home group's last meeting, I was driving my son Jeffrey to middle school when he told me he had a note for me. The devil was behind all those cruel notes that I received at work. The enemy had several puppets working for him who were trying to destroy my husband professionally and our marriage. Immediately, my mind thought that these people were now getting notes to my child. The devil can put some crazy thoughts and ideas in our minds to torment us. My heart sank as wave of nausea came over me because I immediately thought how did they get to my son?

But God had another plan. The Lord used a middle school substitute teacher's note to cut through the darkness in my life and shine his glorious light and love on me. Before I tell you what the note said, think about the odds of that occurring. If a substitute teacher actually took the time to write a note about your child would it be a good note for heaven sakes? It would probably be a bad note. Jeff is a great kid, but he's no angel.

I was so weary from fighting for my marriage and God knew just what I needed. Initially, my energy and desire to fight for my husband was for my children because I didn't want Jeff and Sarah, to go through another divorce. I struggled to put one foot in front of the other each day and breathe, let alone forgive my husband and salvage our marriage. Then God employed a willing substitute teacher to be a life line for a spiritually empty mom who was just trying to hang on for dear life.

As I unfolded a piece of college ruled paper; the note said, "Your son, Jeffrey, is a joy to have in class. He always follows directions and is respectful. He is eager to learn and makes teaching a pleasure. Oh, if only all our students behaved as your son does what a difference it would make in the atmosphere of our school. Thank you for parenting with a purpose." Right at that moment I was undone and wept. I could sense the abundance of God's love right there in my car as I read that divine message from a total stranger.

I knew God was watching me and that he was on my side. It was like God parted the heavens and met me at one of my lowest moments. He was telling me "keep on doing what you are doing, I see you fighting for your marriage and I am with you as you parent with a purpose." That evening our Purpose Driven Life home group met for the last time and I was able to share the note from the substitute teacher.

Due to the shame and my issue with pride, I was still unable to share what was going on in my marriage, but I was able to share what was going on at work and at home with my friend/co-worker Andrea later that evening. She kept my confidences and was a wonderful friend who listened, didn't judge and supported me while I walked through the restoration of my marriage. As I got stronger in the Lord, I was able to be more transparent and our marriage survived that horrible season. I fought the good fight on purpose for my children and then for my husband. Are you living on purpose? Are you making choices that give life to your relationships or are you choosing death?

I've learned that the enemy does his best to convince us that his way is more desirable. Sin opens our lives up to darkness and despair. When we submit ourselves and our troubles to God he lovingly designs a plan and a purpose for our lives even during the most troubling and darkest moments.

Be willing to let him lead, love and equip you for every season of your life. My husband's sin brought destruction; deception and despair to our marriage, but God used it for his glory and our good. I know I am better and stronger for having endured that challenge and for forgiving and loving my husband through it all.

> Your son, Jeffrey, is a joy to have in class. He always follows directions and is respectful. He is eager to learn and makes teaching a pleasure. Oh, if only all our students behaved as your son does, what a difference it would make in the atmosphere of our school. Thank you for parenting with a purpose.
>
> Mrs. LeRoy
> 3-30-04

A MATTER OF FAITH

They replied, "Believe" in the Lord Jesus, and you will be saved you and your household." – Acts 16:31

For many years, I was concerned about my husband's salvation. He believed in God, but wasn't totally convinced that Jesus was the Son of God. As we were going through our rough season in our marriage, I clearly remember running into our church secretary while I was out shopping one afternoon. Behind that happy mask I wore, I remember telling Paula how concerned I was for my husband's salvation. My real concern at the time was how am I going to love and forgive my husband and hang on to our marriage, but I couldn't even begin to tell her what I was really feeling or what I was going through at home.

That afternoon Paula comforted me by sharing Acts 16:31, when she said "Believe Sheri, that you and your household will be saved." Those words not only gave me hope for Jim's salvation but it gave me the strength and courage to hold on for our marriage. Saving our marriage was as important as Jim's salvation. What do you need to believe in the Lord Jesus for? As our marriage got back on the right path, we were in a wonderful honeymoon phase as I started a new career as a high school teacher. Sixty days into my new career is when Jim had a seizure one Sunday morning in our hot tub.

Upon returning home from the grocery store, I heard Jim yelling for help from the backyard. My kids helped me pull him out of the hot tub and call 9-1-1. The EMTs quickly arrived and Jim was able to communicate with us through the entire episode of his seizure. Initially, the EMTs thought Jim was having a panic attack. Later, after X-rays were taken in the emergency room, Jim was diagnosed with stage IV lung cancer that had gone to his brain. As we were heading into surgery, a Florida Hospital representative asked Jim if he wanted prayer and he proudly said "No thank you, my wife has got that covered." I am thankful he had faith in me, but I wanted him to have faith in Jesus. After Jim miraculously recovered from brain surgery, he shared with me what happened to him during his seizure. He told me "I heard a voice as everything appeared brilliantly gold in color when this voice asked me "do you want to live or die?" Jim told me that he said "I want to live." Jim was certain that God asked him that important question right there in our hot tub in the middle of a seizure.

I tell you this because that is what God wants for us. He wants us to live and live abundantly. Even in the darkest days to follow us we lived abundantly. We loved each other like never before and enjoyed the little things in life, like walking hand in hand or taking in all the beauty of nature around us. Through this scary time in our life, I could sense God was really working on Jim's heart. We faced many days of radiation and rounds of chemotherapy. During it all, I was hopeful that Jim would come to know Jesus.

Maybe you, like me, still have family members or friends who have not accepted Jesus Christ as their Lord and Savior. Here is a truth that I hope will give you comfort. God does not have any grandchildren. He only has children. If you are concerned about the salvation of a spouse, a grandparent, friend or a child remember this from Isaiah 48:17 "This is what the Lord says – your Redeemer, the Holy One of Israel: "I am the Lord your God, who teaches you what is best for you, who directs you in the way you should go." God will teach his children.

We were approaching nearly a year of treatments, when one morning

I came home from Jazzercise only to find Jim sobbing as he watched Chuck Norris in an episode of Walker Texas Ranger. I rushed to his side and frantically said "Honey, what's wrong?" He could barely speak when he uttered through the tears "this show!" God's timing is so perfect friend and he knows what it will take to reel us into His Kingdom! On that beautiful September morning, a Christmas episode of Walker Texas Ranger called A Matter of Faith played just for Jim. Jim and I cried together as we watched the final fifteen minutes of the show. That episode beautifully and powerfully presented the true meaning of Christmas – which is that God loves us so much that he sent his son Jesus as an expression of his love and gift for this world and how Jesus died for each of us for the forgiveness of our sins.

That morning while watching a TV program, God used Chuck Norris to lead Jim to accepting Jesus Christ as his Lord and Savior! Jim proudly professed his faith in Jesus Christ three months later to me, my son Jeffrey's grandparents and their pastor during a visit while we were under Hospice Care. Pastor Ron Williams had Jim on his heart for weeks even though he had never met Jim before. Pastor Ron from Palmetto Baptist said to Jim, "it looks like you've provided a beautiful home and life for your family, but if you don't get better do you know where you are going when you die?" Jim said confidently "Yes, I'm going to heaven." And Pastor Ron said "How are you getting there Jim?" Jim said "through my Lord and Savior Jesus Christ."

I've learned that God is at work in the lives of his children no matter how young or old. God knows who you are concerned about. It's a matter of faith friend; believe that God is going to work out the salvation of his children. He loves you and your family so much. You and your household will be saved! That's wonderful news!

DO NOT BE AFRAID

I have given you authority to trample on snakes and scorpions and to overcome all power of the enemy; nothing will harm you. – Luke 10:19

I love Luke 10:19. Jesus tells the disciples that he has given them the authority to overcome all power of the enemy. Jesus is giving us that same authority over everything we face in life. I don't know about you, but I really don't like snakes. Even a dead one can startle me and shake me to my core. Other than an occasional black snake, I have not had many encounters with snakes until 2008, when I started sharing my testimony. Every chance I would get, I would tell people how much Jesus had changed my life. It was a very exciting time for me and I was on fire for the Lord! When you know Jesus loves you and has changed your life, you can't help but tell others. Zeal for Jesus can really upset the devil.

One afternoon, I was being neighborly and was mowing my neighbor's yard when I encountered a coral snake. A couple days later around 7 a.m., my son Jeff had already left the house for school, Sarah and Steven were still sleeping and I was making my way home from walking our dog Bagel around the neighborhood. As I walked up to the house, a coral snake was stretched across the threshold of my front door just lying there daring me to enter my home. I was thinking to myself, are you kidding! I can't even get inside! So I started bombing the snake with pine bark hoping that darn snake would move so I could get in the house and start getting ready for the day. That snake just laid there defiantly unwilling to budge. My lightning fast brain finally had a brilliant idea; grab the water hose. I squirted that snake to get it to move. It took its sweet time but it finally slithered away.

In a panic, I called my friend Laura; she suggested I call Animal Control. Unfortunately, it was too early in the morning for them to help. I had to get Steven up, fed and off to school, and I also had to get ready to lead my bible study. The rest of the morning's routine was off to a rough start and now we're all running late. After dropping Steven off at school, I pulled up in our driveway only to see that snake taunting me as it crawled across my flower bed. I boldly jumped out of my car and courageously declared, "that snake is going down!" I was ready to slay that beast. I kicked off my cute little (who am I kidding, big) sandals and put on my yard shoes and grabbed a shovel.

I stood in my front yard, shovel in hand shaking like a crazy woman, trying to get enough courage to approach and destroy that snake. I cried out, "Oh sweet Jesus you have to help me!" Then I rushed up on that snake and started frantically chopping that bugger up in about eight pieces. My hysterical chopping frenzy left a big hole in my front yard. I roared "Victory" and promptly left my shovel in the ground as a monument to my bravery.

I had been living in my house for over 10 years and other than an occasional black racer I never had encounters with snakes. The devil knows what scares us. He knew that snakes would freak me out. The more I pressed in to knowing God, the more snakes appeared. One night, Steven left the back door open so Bagel could come in and out and a corn snake decided to come in and camp out on my kitchen floor. At first I thought it was a long ribbon. As I was trying to decide how to wrangle that snake, the darn thing crawled into our desk in the kitchen. That was a sleepless night. The next morning that snake was waiting for me across the house by the door to the garage. My hysteria woke up Jeff and he came to my rescue. He said, "Mom calm down, that snake is more afraid of you than you are of it" as he promptly escorted it out the front door. I should have fired my cat.

After that crazy episode with the corn snake I decided to seek some Godly wisdom. Why do these snakes keep showing up? I initially thought that the devil was trying to get to me off track as I pursued God. My friend Trisha shared the bible story about how the Israelites were grumbling and complaining to Moses about everything. The Israelites detested the food and complained that they we're going to die in the desert. The Israelites were big time whiners…do you know a few? Then the Lord sent venomous snakes. Many of the Israelites died from snake bites. I shared this story with all three of my children and suggested that the whining and complaining around the house should cease. Ha! It worked…only for a while. Whining is contagious, even my dogs know how to whine, they learned from my kids.

At the end of that adventurous year, a coral snake appeared in my shower the day of my annual Christmas party. Thankfully, my neighbor came over and he slayed that one. It wasn't too long after that incident that a little black snake curled up next to my central vacuum hose in the hallway one afternoon and he met his untimely death when I sucked it into my vacuum. Another snake took a dip in my pool and I promptly scooped it up and flung over the fence into my neighbor's yard. Several years have passed with no incidents of snakes. Thank you Jesus! Although not too long ago, I had these little tiny snakes appearing in my shower again. I finally discovered that my neighbor had an uncapped sewage pipe in her side yard. I purchased a cap for that pipe and it took care of the problem. Thankfully snakes are no longer appearing in my shower.

I've learned that as we reach new levels with God, sometimes we will face great opposition from the evil one. Friends, the devil doesn't have to spend any time or energy on those who are lost. We're the ones with targets on our backs. God tells us over and over don't be afraid! No fear here. I've got Jesus! God is with us to fight every battle we face, even pesky snakes. I'm still not a fan of snakes but I'm not as fearful as I used to be. I actually had a little snake that lived in my bushes at the car wash for a while, but he's gone now. Remember, God tells us throughout the scriptures not to be afraid. In Joshua 1:9 The Lord says "Have I not commanded you? Be strong and courageous. Do not be terrified; do not be discouraged, for the Lord your God will be with you wherever you go." Trust the Lord, his promises are true, he will always be with us and nothing will harm you, not even snakes!

ANGELS AMONG US

For he will command his angels concerning you to guard you in all your ways. − Psalm 91:11

Before I get into the story, reread that scripture. Did you do it? I hope you did. If you truly believe in the Word of God and trust him, you should rest easier just knowing that God promises to command his angels to guard you in all your ways. I've never seen an angel but I've had encounters that would lead me to believe that God sent someone right at the perfect time when I needed help on several occasions. One day at the car wash a customer came up to me complaining that one of my vacuum cleaners was acting up and cutting off sooner than it should. I opened up the vacuum to see what the problem was...like I knew what I was doing. I had a pretty good idea what it would take to fix it, but I didn't have the right tool to strip one of the wires that looked corroded and loose.

I said a little prayer asking the Lord to bring me someone with a wire cutter/stripper thingy. I didn't know what the tool was called then. Today, I know. It's called a wire stripper. Duh! Right after I prayed, a white van pulled up into one of my car wash bays. I felt a nudge from the Lord to ask my customer if he had the tool I needed. Initially, we had a language barrier but he figured out what I needed. I showed him the problem with the vacuum and he proceeded to fix it for me! I love it when problems like that get resolved so quickly. Thank you Jesus!

Equipment problems normally are fixed quite rapidly, unless you have to order replacement parts. Problems or conflicts with people on the other hand, not so much. It's no surprise that life has its share of problems and we all have them. I can remember one morning; when one of my kids had made a poor decision that left me feeling very frustrated and extremely disappointed. I was fuming mad. I grumbled about the incident all morning over breakfast to my parents, I'm sure they chuckled behind my back after they listened to all my griping and complaining. Welcome to the many challenges of parenting. When your kids are little, they have little tantrums and conflicts that are frustrating but manageable. On the other hand, problems or conflict with teens or adult children are more challenging. I'm thankful that my folks didn't say, "What goes around comes around." I thought this situation was different but it really wasn't. I had done some of the same dumb things. I just didn't get caught. We finished breakfast and I was off to the car wash to get it ready for the weekend.

Thankfully, working at the car wash is very physical so it's a great way to work off some steam and frustration, that way no one gets hurt. I'm kidding, I don't hurt my children. Walking away and taking a breather will not only help you but it will benefit all involved. However, it only takes a second to speak a hurtful word or lash out in anger. I can thankfully say that I held it together really well and nothing was said that I regret. I'm thankful that the Holy Spirit kept my mouth shut…again. One thing I've learned about dealing with conflict is that it's best to keep your peace initially and walk away from the situation. Let the Holy Spirit calm you and orchestrate your next move.

Within seconds of arriving at the car wash I found a silver cluster of angel charms hanging on a foam brush. Each tiny little angel charm was unique and came with a divine message from God just for me. Wink, wink. Peace, Patience and Protection was on the reverse side of each charm. Charming right? God knew exactly what I needed that morning to calm down so I wouldn't wring someone's neck when I got home. Before you rip into someone, take time to blow off some steam with a little hard work or a brisk walk. Take a moment to thank the Lord for being patient with you for all the times you messed up and fell short. Remember, no one is perfect, except Jesus. Pray to the Lord for wisdom and guidance. Wait on the Lord for the right timing and words to speak. When we wait upon the Lord everyone benefits.

It may seem silly, but those little angel charms really spoke to my heart and spirit. God is always trying to speak to us. Some of us (like me) just happen to be hard headed and need the obvious to get our attention. Galatians 5:22 states "But the fruit of the Spirit is love, joy, peace, patience (there's two of the three) kindness, goodness, faithfulness, gentleness and self-control. I know that my self-control kept everyone involved protected. We are instructed in James 4:7 to "Submit yourselves, then, to God. Resist the devil, and he will flee from you." When we submit to the Lord, he is always faithful to take care of our situations and family problems. Submit your conflicts to Jesus, that action alone will eliminate some of the fighting and quarreling in our families.

I've learned that the Holy Spirit will provide everything we need to handle any problem. In this life, we will face family issues, relationship challenges and tough times. When those days come, and they will; we need the Holy Spirit to give us wisdom to handle the problem with grace. It's good to know that my angels were on guard to remind me on that challenging day that I needed an extra measure of peace, patience and protection. Friend, take heart and rest knowing that your angels are guarding you, too.

ASK AND RECEIVE

You do not have, because you do not ask God. – James 4:2b

I don't know about you but sometimes I find I get in a place of desperation long before I call out to the Lord for help. God knows how to speak to us in countless ways. Sometimes he will use something in nature, a sign, or a friend who gives us an encouraging word. The scriptures are packed full of God's wisdom for us. We are his kids and he knows how to reach each of us in our own special way and he can use anything. Since I'm one of his hard headed children, he's been known to use huge signs or the obvious to calm me down or steer me in the right direction.

When my mother doesn't join me at the car wash, I normally spend time alone driving to and from, unless a girlfriend needs a car wash and offers to drive. There are times when I have bigger jobs to do like paint the building or work on the landscaping. As a former public relations and communications professional, the isolation at the car wash has been tough at times and extremely lonely. I'm a people person and now the Lord has me all alone picking up and dumping trash, I could really identify with the story of Ruth as she gleaned the fields. Ruth gleaned wheat and I gleaned pennies and loose change.

One day, on my way to pick up paint at a local hardware store, in my heart I just wanted to know if God even noticed me and saw everything that I was doing all alone. I could feel myself planning a pity party. I was on my way to Ace Hardware when I heard him whisper, "I'm so proud of you Sheri." I felt the love of the Lord, right there in my car. Some of you may need to hear from the Lord too. We don't have because we don't ask. Tell Jesus what you need. Jesus tells us in John 14:13-14 "And I will do whatever you ask in my name, so that the Son may bring glory to the Father. You may ask me for anything in my name, and I will do it." Just ask him anything that's on your heart. That particular day I asked the Lord "Do you see me? And he answered. Maybe you have some questions for the Lord. Do you love me, Jesus? Jesus, will you protect my child or please fix my marriage. In Matthew 21:22 Jesus said to his disciples "If you believe, you will receive whatever you ask for in prayer." Jesus longs to be in close fellowship with you and he wants to answer your prayers.

While working at the car wash, I was also getting serious about my ministry. I attended several Christian seminars; New Year - New You, Living in Your Strengths by Linda Werner and Significant Woman. I was ready to start changing lives and tell people the good news of Jesus Christ. While I was in the middle of Significant Woman, I sensed the Lord saying "when are you going to stop talking about what you want to do and start doing it? Ok Lord, I'll get busy and be intentional. Yes! Intentional. I had some professional brochures printed. Whoo hoo! Five thousand brochures ready to go. Hey, it's cheaper if you purchase more. Please call me, I'll send you some. I think I still have 4,500 left. I started mailing the brochures to various churches in the Central Florida area, family and friends in hopes to have opportunities to share my new passion for saving marriages and sharing my testimony. I was certain that the phone would start ringing. Wrong. Cricket - cricket. Not one call, nothing. I was so frustrated and confused.

One Monday morning, on the way to church to count the offering I cried out to the Lord. Ok, honestly I started whining. I'm an expert at whining; I've learned from my kids. My conversation with the Lord went like this. "Ok Lord, I need a sign. I thought this is what you wanted me to do?" I turned off the radio. I didn't want anything impeding my ability to hear from the Lord. "Hello Lord?" Nothing. Alright, I'll start praying in tongues. My spirit knows how to communicate to the Lord. I actually sing in tongues, so I start singing all the way to church. I'm serious; I need a sign Lord…I'm still singing. As I'm sitting in the intersection just before I crossed the street to pull into the church parking lot, I said to the Lord "Am I in your will, Lord?"

All of a sudden this huge truck pulls next to me getting ready to cross the street in the opposite direction. The truck has these huge letters and this inspiring graphic that read GOD's WILL Through Your Skills and Dedication. Holy Cow! Now that's a sign. The truck wasn't a semi but it was one of those big box trucks.

My spirit and attitude soared. I'm in his will! Immediately, I told my friends about my sign from God. My sweet friend Corrine said "Do you think it was a mirage?" I told her, "I don't care what it was, I saw it and I believe God gave me my sign". A week later, I got my first booking to speak. As time passed, I learned that the truck is a Florida Hospital truck. I have seen that truck from time to time at various locations in Central Florida. Friends would call me and tell me that they've seen "my truck". It still makes me smile just thinking about it. I finally got a good picture of the truck while I was sitting at a traffic light. It's like God brought that truck right to me, to remind me that I'm still in his will. I never want to forget that special moment.

I've learned that the truck actually says God's Work through Your Skills and Dedication but when you're looking for a sign from God, he can change a few little letters to give you the message you're looking for. Matthew 19:26 tells us that "Jesus looked at them and said, "With man this is impossible, but with God all things are possible." All things are possible friend, but remember God does things in his time not ours. You will more than likely have to exercise patience and self-control as you wait on the Lord. The waiting part is not easy. Don't give up. Follow the Holy Spirit. Ask and watch the Lord deliver, that's a promise you can count on.

FIRE!

For our God is a consuming fire. – Hebrews 12:29

When you surrender your life fully to the Lord and start meditating on his word, he becomes this all-consuming fire in your life. I began pursuing the Lord in 2004 when our marriage ran into trouble. I was desperate for power, peace and strength to hold on while we were trying to piece the wreckage of our marriage back together after my husband's infidelity. By studying the word and trusting God, my heart was changed radically. God also changed my husband's heart over many months and then God ultimately restored our marriage. God reignited the fire in our marriage and we were heading to a bright future.

Ten short months after our reconciliation, Jim was diagnosed with Stage IV lung cancer and sadly lost his battle to cancer fifteen months later on New Year's Day of 2007. When Jim died, I really pressed in to know Jesus better by devouring the Word of God. I had been so obedient following his word and was so confused about Jim's illness. I discovered that God is not the author of illness and disease. If God put sickness and disease on us why would we be going to doctors to get well? The enemy is the one who comes to kill, steal and destroy. God loves us. Our bodies are temples of the Holy Spirit and we need to be treating them as temples. My husband smoked for thirty plus years and he didn't manage his stress well. Stress is a killer. You only get this one life and one body. Take care of your body.

After a couple of years of participating in a bible study, I began leading our ladies bible study at church. My speaking opportunities in local churches were growing and I really felt like my ministry was heading in the right direction. Of course, I was still managing the car wash, the home front and the boys. We were preparing to celebrate Jeff's high school graduation when earlier in the week one of my compressors at the car wash was running too long and overheating. I had asked George, (the original owner of the car wash), to check it out and he confirmed that the compressor wasn't shutting off so he switched out compressors and installed our spare compressor.

While we were out celebrating the joyous occasion of my son's graduation, our car wash caught on fire! That's right, the car wash caught on fire. The next day following Jeff's graduation, we were scheduled to hit the road and head to the University of North Florida for summer orientation. George called me the next morning to say that he had to shut down the car wash because most of the equipment melted from the extreme heat.

God gave me such a sense of peace during this tragedy. I calmly called my girlfriends and told them that they didn't need to take care of the car wash over the weekend. They were pretty stunned at how calm I was considering everything that had happened. It makes me think of the profound wisdom found in the Serenity Prayer by Reinhold Niebuhr "God grant me the serenity to accept the things I cannot change, courage to change the things I can and wisdom to know the difference. Living one day at a time, enjoying one moment at a time, accepting hardship as a pathway to peace. Taking as Jesus did, this sinful world as it is, not as I would have it. Trusting that you will make all things right if I surrender to your will so that I might be reasonably happy in this life and supremely happy with you forever in the next, Amen."

There was not one thing I could do to make the situation better at the car wash. It was totally out of my control. I had to trust George to do what he could do and trust God with the rest. Jeff's appointment was the most important thing that I could control so we promptly headed north the very next morning to the University of North Florida for orientation while the car wash smoldered.

Once I returned home, it felt odd that I couldn't go to work at the car wash. It actually took about a month to get everything repaired and running again. I took it upon myself to purchase some new garbage cans at our hardware store when I ran into an acquaintance who knew about my ministry. As she was ringing up my items she smiled and asked me "how's business?" I replied "it caught on fire." Then she said so enthusiastically "that's awesome!" It really made me chuckle. I didn't have the heart to tell her the truth about my car wash so I proudly walked away with a prophetic word for my future. My ministry is going to catch fire!!

I've learned that when the unexpected happens, and it will, God will help us navigate through every twist and turn with power and grace. One of my favorite scriptures is Proverbs 3:5-6. "Trust in the Lord with all your heart and don't lean on your own understanding and in all ways acknowledge him and he will make your path straight." We need to slow down long enough to let God help us. Don't rush to a quick solution. Wait on the Lord by being still and seek him with your whole heart. He promises in his word that when we seek him, we will find him. God will set up the people we need, he will help us through the fire and when it's all said and done, we won't even smell like smoke.

WISDOM

If any of you lack wisdom, he should ask God, who gives generously to all without finding fault, and it will be given to him. – James 1:5

For several years after my husband died, George, who was the original owner of the car wash helped me every Tuesday and Thursday at the business. George was like a father to my husband and he really came to our aid as we were battling cancer. He would take care of the maintenance of equipment or anything that would involve pumps, motors, everything electrical and plumbing. When George turned 83 years old, he told me that it was time for him to hang up his tool belt and he wouldn't be able to help me anymore. I was crushed. It was a very sad day for me because I relied on George all the time. One of the most important things I've learned from owning the car wash is that God wants us to rely on him. He knows what we need and he'll work it out.

Since the car wash is self-service, there is no need to have an attendant during operation hours. I have a note box at the car wash so customers can contact me when a problem occurs. Problems get fixed and money is refunded, unfortunately, most people leave awful notes. Some notes are so nasty that their mother would be embarrassed. Just a side note, don't leave mean notes. One day, I got a note in our note box saying that the rinse cycle didn't work. Usually, the note box has notes where someone lost their money, a vacuum didn't work or the water pressure was low. Getting a note that said "the rinse cycle doesn't work" was a first. Initially, I thought that the customer must be crazy or they don't know how to use the equipment. Of course the rinse cycle works. You have to have a rinse cycle; it's a car wash for the love of Pete.

My mother was 77 years old when this occurred. I would take her to join me frequently so I would not be alone. She was my bodyguard. I read that note and told mom we needed to pray because I did not know how to fix the rinse cycle. I needed some wisdom and needed it quickly. In James 1:5, he writes "if you lack wisdom ask." I prayed "Jesus I need you, please help me, I don't know how to fix the rinse cycle." When I opened up the unit, all I could see was different color wires, screws and a horn. I was in a pickle. Thank the Lord; we have the Holy Spirit to give us wisdom. All we need to do is ask, it's that simple. At that moment, I spoke the most powerful prayer in the whole world, "Jesus help me."

As I was looking at all the wires I heard this soft voice say, "Shut off the power." Oh yeah, shut off the power, so I shut off the power to that bay. As I opened up the control box for that bay, I heard, "Sheri, look at the red wire, it's not hooked to the pink wire." Huh? Now I can't tell you if it was an audible voice but I heard it and that's all I heard. I thought to myself. "Lord, are you trying to tell me how to fix the rinse cycle?" Yes, he was helping me. Jesus is so cool. I unscrewed and stripped the red wire, stripped the pink wire, wrapped them together and secured them under the screw. I turned the power back on, and that rinse cycle worked! Jesus is awesome.

I have learned that when you lean on Jesus he will never let you down. I know this first hand to be true. As I lean on Jesus and study the Word of God, the smarter I become. Who doesn't want to be smarter? Recently I heard Jase Robertson of Duck Dynasty speak at Christ Church in Jacksonville, Florida and he said "the Bible is a Weapon of Mass Instruction." Yes it is. There may come a time when we need instruction or help and it may not be spelled out in the Bible. Here's what you do, call on Jesus and ask him for wisdom. God promises that when you seek him with your whole heart you will find him. All our answers to life's problems are found in Christ Jesus.

TITHE TO TIES

Bring the whole tithe...Test me in this, says the Lord Almighty, and see if I will not throw open the floodgate of heaven and pour out so much blessing that you will not have room enough for it. – Malachi 3:10

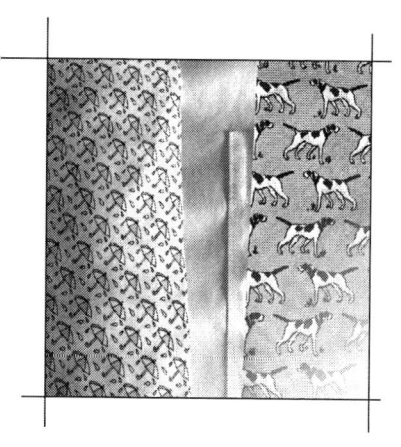

I've always said, "How thankful I am to God that my mom or a friend was with me when crazy situations happened at the car wash." Having a witness lends to my credibility and helps me not look so crazy. Several years ago, our church family was going through the sermon series, called The ABCs of Financial Freedom. My son, Jeff, was going to come into some money for college and I had asked him to let me borrow some of it for a deposit for his brother's braces until I could pay him back. When I got the money, I wondered if I should tithe on that money. I called my friend, Laura, who is my prayer and accountability partner and asked her what she thought. Her advice to me was, "just go into church and listen to our pastor's message." I listened and after hearing several supporting scriptures, I decided I should tithe and I did.

Later that same afternoon, I had a speaking engagement at a local church. My friend Cindy joined me to take care of business at the car wash immediately after our church's service. We changed out of our church clothes and threw on our shorts and drove across town. As soon as we got to the car wash, I headed over to the garbage cans located in front of my business and found a brand new dress shirt with the price tag still on it and two ties! The original price of the shirt was five dollars less than what I tithed that morning. The sales price of the shirt was $69. It was a great looking dress shirt.

Immediately, I thought of my son Jeff. He was obedient to my request for the money and now God is blessing me with a shirt and ties for my boy! God knows that we want to give our children nice things and God wants to give his children nice gifts too. Jesus specifically states in Matthew 7:11 "If you, then, though you are evil know how to give good gifts to your children, how much more will your Father in heaven give good gifts to those who ask him."

My son Jeff is very involved in his fraternity and he loves Brooks Brothers clothes. Brooks Brothers clothing is a bit pricey for momma's pocket book, but not for God's. One of those ties is a Brooks Brothers tie! It is so cute, caramel in color with hunting dogs all over it. I knew my son would love that tie. Jesus knew Jeff would love that tie as much as I would love my Rollins College sweatshirt. I had never even heard of the brand of the other tie but it's a soft pale yellow with umbrellas and tiny little rain drops. It is a precious tie. I thought to myself, I'm going to wrap these items and give them to Jeff for Christmas! Yes, I'm not above wrapping up treasures from the car wash trash can for my kids or my friends. I must add that these three items were pristine, not a mark or a blemish on them even after pulling them out of the trash.

This took place in October, so I took the items home and tucked them away in my closet for safe keeping until Christmas. Jeff came home the following month for Thanksgiving and asked if we could go to one of the Outlet Malls before we head over to the car wash. He wanted to check out a new store that he had heard about so I said "Sure" and we battled

I-4 holiday traffic. We searched high and low for this store called Vineyard Vines. Finally out of desperation, we went to the leasing office only to learn that the store was at Downtown Disney. I looked at Jeff and said "We're done kiddo; we'll go to Downtown Disney over the Christmas break." Jeff was a bit disappointed but said, "Ok mom." Off to the car wash we go.

The next day, I was pressing my sons' shirts for Thanksgiving so they both would look nice. Then I thought to myself "I should pull out that shirt and those ties that I found at the car wash and press them too since I had the iron out...which doesn't happen often." I pressed the shirt and the sweet hunting dog tie. I felt so much joy from the Lord as I was ironing my gifts for my son. Then as I pressed that really cute yellow tie, I turned it over and was stunned. Remember, the store my son and I looked for that we couldn't find? Well that cute tie was a Vineyard Vines tie! From heaven!! God is so amazing. He loves us so much. I came undone when I saw that tie was from Vineyard Vines.

I wrapped up those items in the most beautiful wrapping paper and gave them to Jeff for Christmas that year. Those gifts were the last thing he opened on Christmas morning. I explained the entire story to Jeff through tears of joy before he opened his gifts. I told Jeff how much God loves us and he wants to give us the desires of our hearts. Even in ties! My younger son Steven is so funny; he said "that car wash is like a portal from heaven."

God loves you too. In Philippians 4:19 Paul states "And my God will meet all your needs according to his glorious riches in Christ Jesus." That is one of God's many promises. I have learned to believe and trust God's promises to meet all our needs. Bring God your tithe. The scripture clearly states "Test me." Test God in the area of your finances. Tithing is ultimately a heart issue, when you trust him with all your heart it's easy to trust him with your money. Everything is his anyways. Jesus wants to be intimately involved in every aspect of your life especially your finances. When we trust him whole heartedly with it all, God promises to do immeasurably more than you could ever dream or imagine. Test him and see how much he wants to bless you!

ARE YOU WHO YOU WANT TO BE?

Being confident of this, that he who began a good work in you will carry it on to completion until the day of Christ Jesus. – Phil 1:6

If you're not totally content with yourself, take heart. You are an original and you are exactly who God wants you to be. The good news is that the scriptures promise when we trust him and surrender our life to him, he will keep working on us until Jesus comes back or he brings us safely home. Kristin Armstrong described how God worked on her struggle with pride in her book, Work in Progress, An Unfinished Woman's Guide to Grace, "I had a serious interior renovation project to undertake with no luxury of temporarily moving into a rental…" Friend, God arranges renovation projects in our lives disguised as challenges or people problems to continue the good work in us. One of God's renovation projects on me happened about five years after my husband had died. It was an average day, getting Steven up and to school, walking the dog, working out at the gym and then off to the car wash to take care of business. In the afternoons, I would check emails and take care of the endless chores around the house and yard.

This particular afternoon, I got a troubling email request from a relative. The request was going to cost me a hefty sum financially. I struggled with the request, so did everyone I complained to about it. I won't give all the details because that part doesn't matter and I would rather protect all those involved. What matters is how God used this huge challenge in my life to see if I was just a fan of Jesus or was I a true follower. It took me days of prayer and sleepless nights to decide on what to do. I was in such turmoil and didn't have any peace about the request. I even called for prayer from a ministry that I support. I was desperate for some Godly wisdom because what I was hearing from those closest to me did not give me peace at all. The caring man who took my call asked me "What did I need to trust God for?" I never even thought of my situation in those terms. I was more focused on what the request was going to cost me and my family. God already knew the situation and all of the details. God was waiting for me to seek his guidance and wisdom. In the natural, this just seemed so big, daunting and would ultimately hurt me and my children financially.

While I was struggling with this financial request, my mind was reeling with horrible thoughts that were rooted in fear, anger, disappointment...oh I could go on and on. One morning as I was taking Steven to school I heard Switchfoot's song, playing on the radio, This is your life are you who you want to be? I could feel the Holy Spirit working on me and stirring me up. "No, I thought. This is not who I want to be!" I don't like the way I'm feeling. I don't like the awful thoughts racing through my head. The Holy Spirit was tugging at me. Sheri, who are you going to trust? Are you going to trust me the great I AM or your bank accounts? Who's your source Sheri? Is your source your financial portfolio or the Prince of Peace?

As soon as I arrived home, I took the dog for a walk and was several blocks from home in the neighborhood that connects to our neighborhood. The sidewalks in Wekiva are located behind the backyards and most are lined with privacy fences. A section of our walk is like walking through a labyrinth. As I made the turn through the fenced line maze there is a large green power box tucked in the corner and I saw that someone (an angel perhaps or Jesus himself) wrote in chalk "Is this the life you want?" As crazy as that sounds, it's true. Some of us need the obvious. Thankfully, it wasn't a 2 x 4 up the side of my head. I say that jokingly. God is gentle and kind. He's not going to hurt or punish you ever.

God really knows how to reach my heart. I didn't want to feel those negative feelings any more. As soon as I saw that message on the power box, I knew I had to write that check and put the situation to bed. More importantly I needed to trust God with my fears and taking care of all my financial needs. God is our source. He will take care of everything when we seek him and not lean on our own understanding. God tells us in 1 Peter 5:7 "Cast all your anxiety on him because he cares for you." In Philippians 4:6 - Paul tells us "Do not be anxious about anything, but in everything, by prayer and petition, with thanksgiving present your requests to God. And the peace of God, which transcends all understanding, will guard your hearts and minds in Christ Jesus."

I've learned not to focus so much on my problems or the situations at hand but focus on God's promises. God promises in Jeremiah 29:11 "For I know the plans I have for you," declares the Lord, "plans to prosper you and not to harm you, plans to give you hope and a future." God is calling us to live a very different life. We often look at the natural consequences instead of the promises of God's supernatural blessings. In Philippians 4:19 Paul tells us that God promises to "supply all our needs according to his riches and glory in Christ Jesus." He knows what concerns us. Tell God your concerns, ask for his help and he will take care of it. The Holy Spirit will always lead you to the best solution. This is your life, are you who you want to be?

YOU ARE LOVED!

I have loved you with an everlasting love; I have drawn you with loving kindness. – Jeremiah 31:3

I have owned my car wash for over 18 years and at the beginning of 2013, I was in the middle of negotiations to sell the business. The car wash had always been my husband's dream and his plan to have something to do when he retired. It was never my dream. Part of me was really ready to let it go, and another part of me was so unsure of leaving that part of my life behind and stepping fully out into the unknown. I was in my fifth year of running it on my own when I finally got an offer for the business.

One afternoon, I made a quick stop at the car wash to check on things before I headed to my friend's house to meet his family. As I finished dumping the trash, I noticed a post-it note with the message "You are loved" with a heart drawn on it stuck to the bottom of the trash can. The note was perfect, not a spot on it. It was like it was placed there immediately after I dumped the trash. I've told this story several times and the frequent question is did your boyfriend put it there? The crazy thing is if he did, how would he get it to stick on the bottom of the can? The garbage can was full of trash when I dumped it. What are the odds of it staying at the bottom or falling in the trash with the rest of the garbage? Besides, I asked and he didn't place the post-it note at the bottom of the garbage can.

This is what I do know, God is love and he loves us so much. I think he knows just when I need to hear from him. That same week I was cutting up my strawberries to put on my cereal only to see a heart right in the middle of a strawberry. It wasn't too long after that situation that my teenage son Steven wrote God loves you on a tiny post-it note at the house. Now that's a miracle. Like I mentioned earlier, I'm a people person. I love being around people. As a public affairs and communications professional of a major telecommunications company for 16 of my 21 years of service, I felt like a fish out of water working at the car wash. God took those years of isolation at the car wash and used that valuable time to work on my relationship with him. I could really identify with Ruth from the Old Testament. I'm widowed and thought I would never meet a godly man let alone meet him at my car wash.

Joyce Meyer said once that "God can drop a man in your driveway." It's true. I had tried several of the online dating sites. The online dating experience was kind of like fishing for me. If there isn't any activity it can be painfully boring. It wasn't for me. My girlfriend and I were replacing a vacuum motor and an air line hose at the car wash one morning. Honestly, we looked like a modern day version of Lucy and Ethel. The morning repairs were going pretty smoothly despite dropping a brand new vacuum motor from the top of a 10 foot ladder. I prayed the blood of Jesus over that motor and praise God it still worked. Then we had to connect an air line hose. We just didn't have the dexterity or strength to connect the air line, then help arrived.

My sweet customer, who is now a friend, showed up at the perfect time.

God bless that man. Donnie is one of my customers at my car wash. We spent several years just being acquaintances. Randomly, we would see each other and have wonderful conversations. We learned that we were both born again believers and we agreed politically. Our friendship was off to a good start and now I needed his help.

Donnie stood over the foam brush equipment for hours that morning and wasn't about to leave until everything was working properly. My girlfriend said that I owed him dinner. Oh no, I thought, that is not my mode of operation. I do not take men out for dinner. She insisted so I bravely told him "my girlfriend says I owe you dinner." He agreed, we had a great time and became friends. After several months, I learned that Donnie was a contractor. He can fix anything! God knew just what I needed and he knows just what you need too. Donnie worked for me for almost a year when one day he asked me to lunch and then a movie.

The rest is still yet to be written, but we are engaged! Our relationship is so different and much better because we are committed to keep Christ in the center. We honor God and each other. If you're single and looking, trust God's timing. I've learned that we need to keep our hearts open to the possibilities God has for us. God knows what's best. You are loved by the Lord and he has a great plan for your life. If you're married and your marriage needs some help give your concerns to Jesus. Jesus can fix up, tune up and restore any relationship. Remember you are loved!

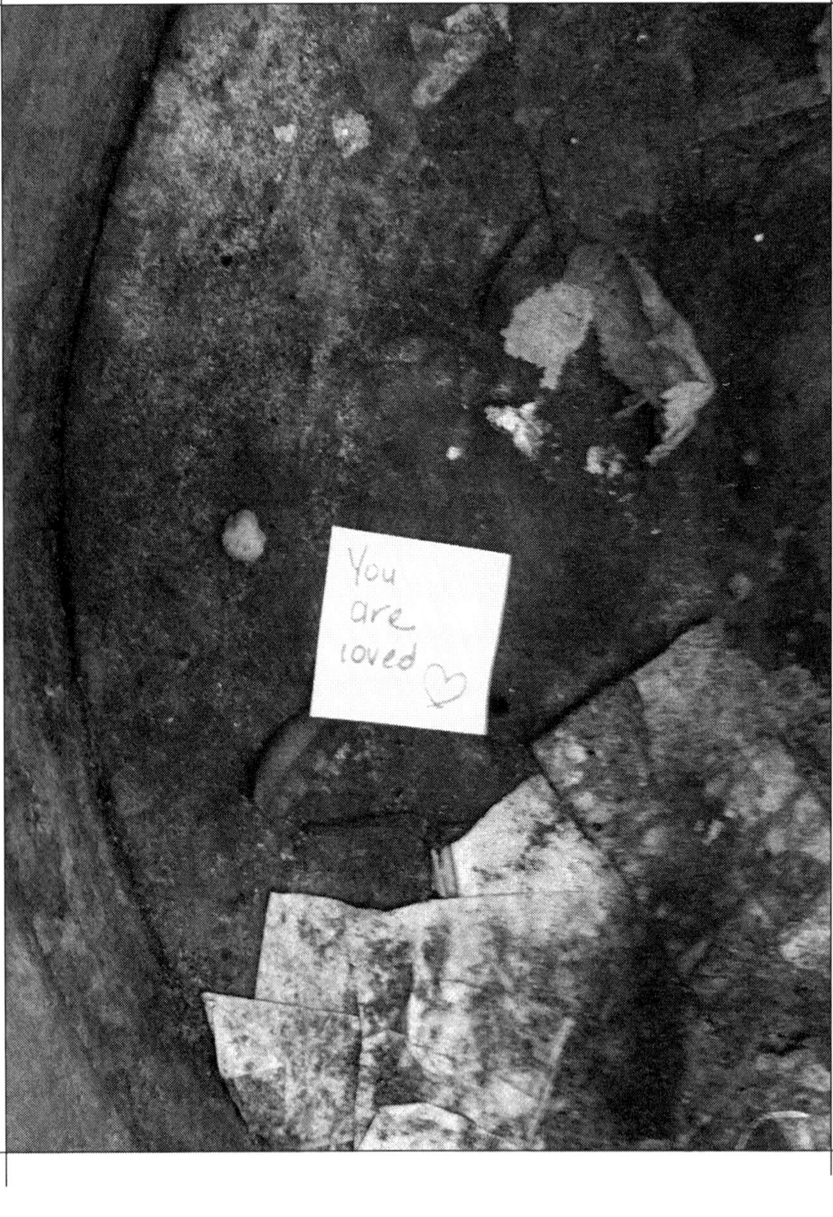
You
are
loved

BLESSED!

Whoever gives heed to instruction prospers; and blessed is the one who trusts in the Lord. − Proverbs 16:20

I don't know about you but I want to be blessed, from Genesis to Revelation, God continues to tell us over and over again to follow my word, give heed to my instruction, trust me, bless others in my name and I will bless you. I have been blessed by family and friends who have trusted in the Lord. I'm so thankful for the prayers of my parents, grandparents, aunts, uncles and friends. I know their prayers have ushered me to where I am today. If you have family and friends who will pray for you, you are blessed. If you don't, please join a body of believers who will meet you where you are and love you into the everlasting arms of Jesus.

When my marriage with Jeffrey's dad was falling apart, my friend and co-worker Jamie was the first person who prayed with me with such passion and authority. Her love for Jesus was contagious. Her passion set me on a course to have a deeper relationship with God. We've been blessed to remain great friends for over 20 years. I watched her take a giant leap of faith back in the early 90's when she left her career to stay home with her first child. As time marched on she lived counter culture to all my other friends by staying home with her kids. The rest of us went back to the work force after we had our children. Jamie, on the other hand, continued to have her babies and then home schooled them. I don't say this to judge the working mom because many of us don't have a choice. My husband and I made the choice for me to work during most of our children's life. The good news is that when we trust in the Lord and follow his word he will bless us right where we are at.

God reminded me again that he will bless me if I trust him. Jamie and I went shopping to get a jump on our Christmas list at this cute store called the Peddler's Wagon in downtown Eustis, Florida. It's a store with beautiful unique home décor items and gifts. I was drawn to these little pear candles. They were so sweet. Jamie and I continued browsing through the store and looking at all the beautiful Christmas decorations. Delicious hors d'oeuvres and punch were served that day, talk about being blessed. We felt like royalty. Wait, we are royalty! We're daughters of the King! I couldn't resist and purchased those sweet little pear candles, three to be exact.

Later in the week, one of the tasks on my endless to-do list was to clean out my shed in the back yard. I had several boxes to go through from my short lived career as high school teacher. My goal was to bless my son's English teacher with some books for her library, items for her classroom ranging from inspirational posters to various classroom supplies and organize my shed. As I was going through the boxes that had been tucked away for nearly eight years, I came across a note pad still wrapped in cellophane. This little note pad had three pears at the top of the pad and they looked just like the pear candles I had purchased. Across the bottom of the note pad was Proverbs 16:20 paraphrased "Blessed is He who trusts in the Lord."

Over that weekend, I was at the Maitland Art Festival with my sweetheart and I saw this cool watercolor of a pear that caught my attention. It was like getting a nudge from Jesus and the Holy Spirit all over again. Do you remember the scripture I gave you this week Sheri? Yes, Lord. I know that when I heed your instruction you will prosper me and when I trust you Lord, you will bless me. The same promise is for you too. By now you know that God speaks to me in various ways. Friend, he's trying to do the same for you. I pray that your spiritual eyes, ears and heart will be opened so you can hear and see God. His ways to communicate to us are unlimited.

This is one of my favorite scriptures that reinforce the message of how much God wants to bless us. In this amplified version of Psalm 1:1-3 David clearly tells us what to avoid and how we should live to be blessed by God. "Blessed (happy, fortunate, prosperous, and enviable) is the man who walks and lives not in the counsel of the ungodly (following their advice, their plans and purposes), nor stands (submissive and inactive) in the path where sinners walk, nor sits down (to relax and rest) where the scornful (and the mockers) gather. But his delight and desire are in the law of the Lord, and on His law (the precepts, the instructions, the teachings of God) he habitually meditates (ponders and studies) by day and by night. And he shall be like a tree firmly planted (and tended) by the streams of water, ready to bring forth its fruit in its season; its leaf also shall not fade or wither; and everything he does shall prosper (and come to maturity)". That's a powerful scripture to meditate on day and night.

I've learned over the past twenty years that the more you seek God through his word and follow his ways; you will discover his love for you. He longs to bless his children in various ways. Study the word; seek to know the Lord with all your heart and you will find him. He promises that we will find him in Jeremiah 29:13-14 "You will seek me and find me when you seek me with all your heart. I will be found by you, declares the Lord." Seek him friend and he will bless you in countless ways.

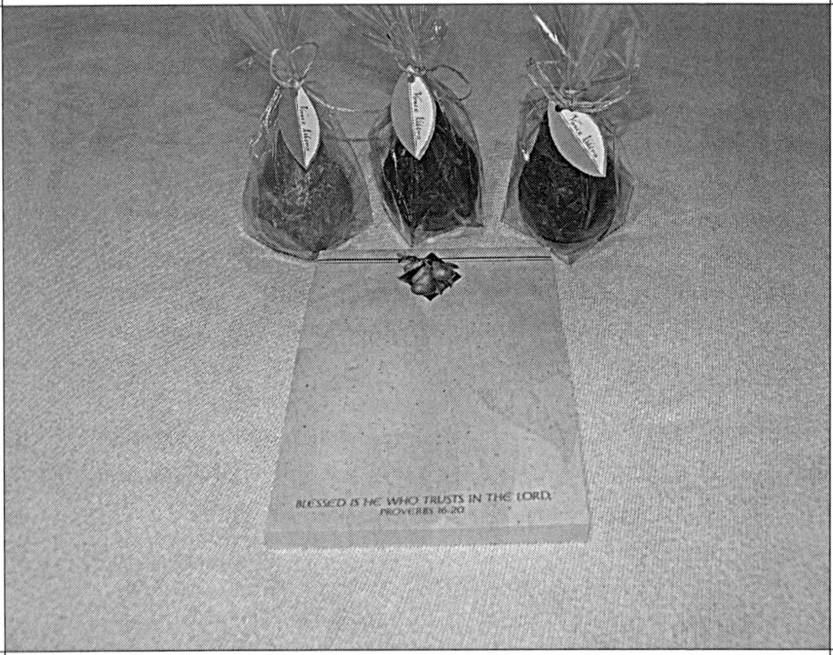
BLESSED IS HE WHO TRUSTS IN THE LORD.
PROVERBS 16:20

3:16

It's Time

For God so loved the world that he gave his one and only Son, that whoever believes in him will not perish but have everlasting life. – John 3:16

In 2012, I was waiting for an offer to come in for the purchase of my car wash. Yes, it was time to let the business go. The Lord knew that I was ready for a change and thankfully God was getting ready to do something new in my life. Several of my closest girlfriends told me for years that I should write a book. God knew my desires to share the good news of the gospel and he had my friends encourage me to write. After only a few months of dating Donnie, I shared with him that I felt like the Lord wanted me to write and my girlfriends had been telling me the same thing. After I got an offer for the car wash, Donnie offered to run the car wash for me through the end of 2013.

Studying the scriptures has become my favorite thing to do every morning. One day, I came across Luke 3:16 which is Luke's account of Jesus being baptized by John the Baptist. John answered them all, "I baptize you with water. But one who is more powerful than I will come, the straps of whose sandals I am not worthy to untie. He will baptize you with the Holy Spirit and fire." I thought Wow, that's a powerful scripture! Most people know John 3:16 but I wonder what the other 3:16 scriptures have to teach us? The more 3:16 scriptures I studied, the more excited I got and my writing adventure began.

God wanted me to study and write a book on all the 3:16 scriptures. I shared my exciting revelation with Donnie, and he said firmly "I'll take care of the car wash; you get busy doing what God is calling you to do." Donnie graciously offered to run the business for me for several reasons. First, I had been working almost daily at this car wash for 18 years; I really needed to be weaned off the business. The most important reason was he wanted me to fully dedicate my time to pursue what God was calling me to do.

After I looked at a few 3:16 scriptures in the New Testament, I decided to start at the beginning with Genesis. The entire writing process was fairly easy and other times challenging. The Old Testament was certainly more challenging. I continued to seek God daily and be led by the Holy Spirit and literally had most of the book done faster than I ever dreamed possible. Remember with God nothing is impossible!

What was interesting is the more progress I made writing; the devil was relentless in trying to discourage me along the way with his lies. For months, Donnie was the only person who knew that I was writing. I wasn't sure what friends and family would say if I told them I was writing a book. Besides the devil was having enough fun tormenting me all on his own, I didn't want him using anyone close to me to derail my dream or discourage me.

One morning, I really wanted confirmation from God that I was doing what he called me to do. While walking my dogs around the block, I was praying in the spirit. My dogs stopped to do their business and the Lord put right in front of me - my neighbor's mailbox, # 316. It's like God lovingly patted me on the head and said "yes, Sheri, this is what I want you to do." Later, that day I was so encouraged and excited! God inspired me to press on. I've never written so much in my life. I have had my share of assignments for high school, college and writing presentations for my ministry, but this was different. I knew this was the Lord's will and he was working through me.

As time marched on I was really making progress and feeling really good about how much I had accomplished. I still had not shared what I had been working on with any of my friends and old "red legs" a/k/a the devil would show up again trying to beat me up mentally with his old worn out script of lies. I found myself seeking the Lord for confirmation just… here we go again, one more time. God is so faithful to be patient with me. As I sat at a traffic light, on my way to the gym one morning, I asked the Lord again "Is this 3:16 book really what you want me to do?" As soon as I looked up, the car right in front of me had a Florida tag with the numbers 316 and three letters. Thank you Jesus!

If that weren't enough, later for reinforcement that night, my phone started tweeting and beeping as I was telling Donnie about seeing the 316 license plate. My friend Cristy sent me a text message; and a picture as we were sitting in the food court at the mall. Cristy's text message read "Just saw this in the parking lot at Publix and it made me think of you." The picture was a huge RV. You're probably thinking, what is so special about an RV? This RV had a powerful message covering both sides that read "God loves you! So get used to it!" John 3:16. Cristy's text message continues with "they have a message over the door of the RV that says "Come on in and let's talk about Jesus." At that very moment, I literally came undone and wept in the food court.

Ask, seek and knock. God will answer. God used someone's ministry to catch the eye of a friend, who in turn would think of me. God knows me so well. He knows you too. I have seen that RV on numerous occasions and it always makes me smile. My friend Carey lovingly calls that RV my mother ship. Hopefully, someday I'll be able to meet the owner of that RV and share how God used their ministry to inspire me and keep me going.

I've learned that when God calls us to do something it may seem too difficult to accomplish in our own ability or with the gifts and talents he's given us. Philippians 2:13 Paul says, "For it is God who works in you to will and to act according to his good purpose." He wants us to fully rely on his power at work in us to complete his good and pleasing purpose in our life. God's power that is at work in us can do immeasurably more than we could ever dream or imagine. Don't quit or give up on what God is calling you to do. Dream big friend, dream big.

EPILOGUE

I hope you've enjoyed my stories from my car wash days. As you can see people and life can be messy just like our cars. The good news is we have a loving savior who will gently wash, wax and clean us up; he will even vacuum all the debris that rattles around on the floor boards of our hearts and lives if we just invite him into our hearts. My car wash business days are over and I thank God for all the valuable lessons and his promises I have learned over the past eighteen years. I was once a worn out and lost wife, mother, daughter, and business professional who was trying to please everyone in my performance based life. Now, I'm a woman free in Christ! My goal in life is to inspire others to love, forgive and build strong families. I know that I can do all things, (the good, bad, ugly and the messy) through Christ who strengthens me and you can too.

I've learned that God is right there with us this very moment no matter where we are, what challenge or heartbreak we're facing. He was with me all the time at my little car wash business and I know that he will be with me until I'm ushered into his loving arms when he calls me home. I am so happy for my new life in Christ! Take that step and invite him in to your heart. It will change your life in amazing ways.

If you made the decision to accept Jesus or you have rededicated your life to him, I would love to hear from you! I can be contacted through my website at www.sheriaustin.net, email, Facebook and on Twitter @sherija2.